ARTIST TRANSCRIPTIONS® BASS

Ray Brown

Legendary Jazz Bassist

Note-For-Note Transcriptions of 18 Classic Performances

by Matthew Rybicki

ISBN 978-1-4584-1242-3

HAL•LEONARD®
CORPORATION

7777 W. BLUEMOUND RD. P.O. BOX 13819 MILWAUKEE, WI 53213

Visit Hal Leonard Online at
www.halleonard.com

For Bob, Gladys, Jim, and Mike Rybicki

FOREWORD

"Of ability, quality or eminence considerably above the normal or average." That's the definition of "great," according to the *Oxford English Dictionary*. It's also a perfect description of the playing of Raymond Matthews Brown.

From the mid-1950s until his untimely death in 2002, every major, celebrated bassist from Sam Jones to Ron Carter to Buster Williams to John Clayton to John Patitucci and everyone in between has listed Ray Brown as a primary influence. Brown's playing exemplified the very best of all aspects of bass playing—sound, time, technical fluidity, intonation, harmonic intelligence, and most of all, *groove*! I once heard a highly respected drummer say, "It was hard to play with Ray Brown, because he grooved and swung so forcefully, drums were somewhat superfluous. He was a one-man band."

Kudos to the wonderful bassist, Matthew Rybicki, for his thorough research and giving us these figurative maps of harmonic greatness from Ray Brown. I urge you to purchase the recordings from which these transcriptions are derived, so you can not only read the notes, but most importantly, feel the groove of Mr. Raymond Matthews Brown.

Enjoy,

Christian McBride

Ray Brown

CONTENTS

"Ray Brown is probably one of the greatest talents ever on his particular instrument. He has a natural, intuitive feel for anything he approaches musically, and his sound is so huge and personal that listeners recognize it almost automatically."

- Oscar Peterson

"He's the greatest working bass player I know. He's done more of it and he's done it well. He's a complete bass player and soloist."

- Milt Hinton

"Ray Brown is the reason I play bass. The instrument chose me and I chose Ray Brown. At age sixteen, I didn't know much about how awesome he was, but the more I studied him and studied with him, the more I learned what the jazz world already knew: he was a pivotal force in jazz from his bebop days until his death."

- John Clayton

"I have a special place for Ray Brown's playing because his approach to the instrument was the thing that inspired me initially ... [he] is the fundamental influence that I have on my playing. He kind of holds a special place for me."

- Dave Holland

"He developed a lot of the skills that became the standards of the next generation of virtuoso bassists. Like Blanton, Mingus, and Pettiford, Ray developed his technique before the invention of amplifiers and metal strings ... He knew how to project his tone ... making the bass line powerfully propel the rhythm section and the band."

- Bill Crow

"Ray has an insatiable desire—insatiable, absolutely insatiable—to find the right note at the right time ... [He is] the epitome of forethought; sympathetic forethought."

- Oscar Peterson

"Ray had so much love of life and the music. He had so much integrity. He treated the music with so much dignity and respect. I spent four and a half years as a sideman with Ray Brown's trio. Music was his life, more so than anyone I could mention."

- Benny Green

"Mr. Brown was 'Mr. Bass,' that's it! When I first heard him play in 1943 I said to myself, 'Good God! This man comes from another planet!' I had never heard a bass played like that. And he swung so hard."

- Hank Jones

"Ray was the man! He got the biggest and strongest sound ever on the bass. His sound came directly from the center of the earth. Like an earthquake."

- Lionel Hampton

"Ray Brown is on every recording date I ever do—if I can get him. He's simply the best there's ever been."

- Quincy Jones

INTRODUCTION

Ray Brown is a legend of jazz bass, and his playing is considered by many to be the standard by which all other bassists are judged. It is with the same respect and admiration that I present this book.

During the course of this work, I realized that no one had written anything specifically focused on Ray Brown. This seemed odd given the fact that he was one of the most prolific jazz bassists ever, and was an undisputed master of the instrument. Perhaps it is that he had been too prolific—where does one start in trying to quantify or qualify such a master? For that matter, why would anyone want to? Why not just enjoy?

While I agree that we should enjoy his work, we can learn just as much from it. Not only can we learn technical specifics, but we can also learn from his incomparable musicianship. Such an undeniably great artist, whose career spanned the greater part of jazz history, is unquestionably deserving of our attention. In that spirit, I assembled this book for all musicians so that we may appreciate, understand, and get closer to some of Ray's significant works.

There are so many recordings to draw from that one could conceivably transcribe for years and not finish his entire discography. My intent with this book is to give the reader a general feel for the different phases of Ray's career, focusing on significant recordings and artists he played with, as well as many of the "Ray-isms" that helped make him so unique.

This book is geared primarily toward bassists, though any performer is sure to gain much from studying these recordings. There is no substitute for personally listening, studying, and playing through the bass lines and solos of the masters.

In general, I have omitted articulations, as listening is the key to learning the nuances of this beautiful music. Jazz is an aural art form and so must be learned in large part by ear. To that end, the compact disc titles and catalog numbers are listed on the first page of each transcription.

I strongly encourage you to purchase the recordings and listen intently before, during, and after your study. It is extraordinarily important to note that in order to be able to understand, assimilate, and perform this music we must go to the masters first. Any time that you can use your eyes *and* your ears to learn, you will benefit much more than reading printed music alone.

Finally, I cannot say enough how helpful it is to memorize these bass lines and solos— even the long pieces. You will benefit greatly from your own hard-won successes in learning how Ray did what he did.

Of course, enjoy, and as the jazz masters say: "Straight ahead and strive for tone."

Matthew Rybicki

BIOGRAPHY

Raymond Matthews Brown was born in Pittsburgh, Pennsylvania, on October 13, 1926. His father, a chef, filled the house with the music of Fats Waller, Duke Ellington, Art Tatum, and Count Basie. Ray received his first formal musical training on the piano when he was eight years old—about the time he started attending Duke Ellington and Count Basie concerts—and later learned to play the bass by ear.

Shortly after his high school graduation, Brown went on the road with the Jimmy Hinsley Sextet and traveled with the group for six months. The following year he joined the Snookum Russell band, playing larger clubs throughout the United States. In 1945, Ray moved to New York City where he heard the greatest talents in the jazz world play, and quickly took his place alongside them.

Immediately upon Ray's arrival in New York, pianist Hank Jones introduced him to Dizzy Gillespie, who invited him to "sit in" at a rehearsal the next day. Diz liked Ray's playing so much that day that he hired him on the spot, and kept him in his band for two years. Performing with Dizzy, Charlie Parker, Max Roach, and Bud Powell, Ray became the premier bassist in the new art form of bebop.

After leaving Diz's band, Ray formed his first trio in 1948 with Hank Jones and drummer Charlie Smith. During those early "big band" years, he became involved with Norman Granz's Jazz at the Philharmonic, and became a regular member of the JATP tour in 1949. This relationship proved fruitful in several ways, most notably in that Ray met fellow JATP members Ella Fitzgerald (whom he later married) and pianist Oscar Peterson while in the band. Ray became a longtime member of Oscar's famous trio, and the group worked steadily until 1966. Ray credited his association with Peterson for a great deal of his success, and their trio remains an example of brilliant music, real communication, and camaraderie.

Ray settled in Los Angeles, California, in 1966 and immediately became the most requested studio bassist in town. He recorded there with a wide variety of musical greats, from Louis Armstrong to James Brown, and from Leonard Bernstein to Aretha Franklin. He was the bassist for Frank Sinatra's television specials, and worked with other stars like Joey Bishop, Red Skelton, the Smothers Brothers, and Merv Griffin.

In the 1960s Ray composed "The Gravy Waltz," which won him a Grammy Award and later became the theme song for *The Steve Allen Show*. Ray continued to record and worked as a manager of several artists including The Modern Jazz Quartet. He produced, taught music, helped write four hundred scores for film and television, and became a champion for California musicians. He created his own company, Ray Brown Music, and even developed and constructed his own cello design.

The 1970s proved equally busy for Brown. In 1972 he recorded a long overdue session with Duke Ellington entitled *This One's for Blanton* in which he paid homage to Ellington's late bassist Jimmy Blanton. Ray deeply admired Blanton and cited him as his primary influence on the bass. In 1974 Ray, drummer Shelley Manne, saxophonist and flautist Bud Shank, and guitarist Laurindo Almeida formed another outstanding group called the L.A. Four, which recorded frequently. Throughout the decade, Ray continued to produce, manage, record, and teach. He organized concerts at the Hollywood Bowl, and was the musical director for both the Monterey and Concord Jazz Festivals.

In the early 1980s, Brown once again teamed up with former Oscar Peterson Trio guitarist Herb Ellis, and formed a trio called Triple Treat with Jamaican-born pianist Monty Alexander. In 1984, Ray formed the new Ray Brown Trio with pianist Gene Harris and drummer Jeff Hamilton. They remained together for nine years, until 1994 when the young pianist Benny Green replaced Harris, and eventually drummer Greg Hutchinson joined the group.

Later, pianist Larry Fuller and drummer Karriem Riggins comprised the working members of the Ray Brown Trio, and Ray continued performing, recording, touring, and teaching all over the world.

During his lifetime, Ray Brown received virtually every major award in jazz, including the National Endowment for the Arts' Jazz Master Award, numerous DownBeat Readers Poll Awards, multiple Grammy Awards, and countless others.

On July 2, 2002, while on tour in Indianapolis, Indiana, Ray Brown died in his sleep. His legacy remains powerful, and he is deeply missed.

TRANSCRIBING TOOLS

Many devices, applications, and techniques were used for this transcribing project. The equipment included a JVC XL-M407 CD player, Onkyo TX-8211 power amplifier, Panasonic SA-AK17 shelf stereo system, Tascam CD Bass Trainer CD-BT2, *Amazing Slow Downer* and *Transcribe!* software, Bose AE2 headphones, Klipsch Custom-2 in-ear, noise-isolating earphones and full-quality ("lossless") digital recordings when CDs were not in use. For digital files, I ran iTunes 11.0.4 on an iMac with OSX 10.8.

When transcribing the songs, I first played along with the recordings. When necessary, I isolated sections, looped them, often changed octaves, and listened at various speeds. I sometimes used a spectrum analyzer to isolate bass notes as well. I should mention that some of these techniques can provide false notes, and I strived to confirm questionable sections in multiple formats.

It is also important for me to bring to your attention that there are a handful of notes that are truly unclear. I did my best to capture exactly what I heard, and avoided writing my own choices or notes that may have made more "sense" harmonically.

Additionally, I enlisted several first-rate bassists to check these transcriptions and provide me with feedback and corrections. I am very grateful for their help.

Lastly, I used Finale 2011 to notate the pieces and was able to synchronize the recordings with the Finale playback when checking passages that were exceedingly difficult to notate or play along with.

Matthew Rybicki

SONG NOTES

Autumn in New York

In this relaxed ballad sung by Ella Fitzgerald and Louis Armstrong, notice how Ray plays mostly half notes. Additionally, there is little embellishment in his bass line, making this performance a bit reserved. This was likely a conscious decision by Ray so as not to distract from the vocals being the primary focus on the recording.

As the arrangement travels through the two keys, pay attention to the feeling that Ray evokes, as well as to his repetition of ideas. This song is just one example (of many) of his playing that debunks the myth that good bass lines should never repeat themselves within a tune. Of special note are his answers to the musical events in measures 17–18, 50, and 54.

Lastly, note the sound of the instrument and the rhythmic feeling that Ray demonstrates, particularly the warm and woody tone and the strong time that shines through. These elements play a part in anchoring the ensemble with purpose and cohesion and generously serve the overall music, rather than Ray's own virtuosity.

Custard Puff

This composition, written by Ray, has some clever arranging devices. Although it uses a traditional 12-bar blues form, Ray plays the melody in only the first eight bars, allowing the guitar to finish the last four. This quickly brings the listener's attention to the form and demands closer inspection.

The "send-off" exchange with the drums (measures 33–44) is a creative way to add interest with a small trio ensemble, and the interlude-like false ending (measures 117–125), complete with an odd number of bars, creates a compelling feeling of suspension.

Ray's 16th-note pull-off device (measures 8, 10, 12, and 14) serves as the main substance of the melody and is a technique that he often incorporated into his performances (several transcriptions in this book include this device). What is particularly creative here is that he chose to take a phrase that is normally used as an ornament and make it the foundation of the melody.

There are two prime examples of a rhythmic technique that almost always produces exciting results: purposefully avoiding the downbeat of strong measures and entering later (measures 45 and 60). This creates quick tension and release and really pushes the momentum of the time forward.

Ray's articulations during his solo (measures 81–104) are full of scoops, slides, and slurs that add a very vocal-like quality to his phrases. There is an almost "slippery" feeling to his musical statements, which compliments the whole piece very well.

Days of Wine and Roses

As a leader, Ray Brown sustained the highest quality of performance through his arrangements. This version of the popular "Days of Wine and Roses" navigates through two keys and employs rhythmic "hits" that add a great amount of interest to the song. Through these devices, Ray effectively created a big-band sound in a trio setting.

There are strong examples of another construction device that Ray used: lines that ascend quickly to the higher register and then suddenly "drop" to a lower register (measures 34–35 and 194–195). I call this device "clef diving." This is especially effective in creating tension and release, and Ray used this concept often.

Ray executes another great solo here filled with musical questions and answers that prove very satisfying (measures 125–128 and 141–148). Notice all of the scoops, hammer-ons, slides, and various other articulations that give his lines color, interest, and a human sound.

In general, this track should serve to remind us that paying attention to the so-called "small" details of arranging can provide terrific results.

Easy Does It

This classic composition was performed regularly by the Oscar Peterson Trio and Ray's own groups. It demonstrates the "intensified nonchalance" that is crucial to swing; the rhythmic attitude on this recording has the perfect mix of relaxation and intensity.

Listen to the bass line in the very beginning. Ray presents a continuous, musical, logical, and swinging line that starts in the high part of the bass register and travels all the way down to the basement via the lowest note on the instrument. Additionally, listen as he navigates through the next few bars to his starting note and comes back down once again (measures 1–16).

Contrast all of this with the last melody chorus (measures 65–70), where he chooses to remain in the high register of the bass. Notice the sense of suspension that is created by the register he chooses, rather than by the harmony or the rhythm. This is a wonderful example of how effective playing goes beyond simply choosing the right notes.

Gravy Waltz

Ray Brown was deeply connected to many parts of the music industry. He was, of course, a first-rate bassist, but also was a producer, contractor, manager, and composer, among other things. His best-known composition, this song was used as the theme for *The Steve Allen Show*, a television variety program that aired in the '50s and '60s.

In this trio recording with Oscar Peterson, notice how the broad rhythmic choices that Ray makes over several choruses help to gradually alter the feeling of the music over time. During the statement of the melody, he generally stays close to the repetitive rhythm established in bar 41 (measures 41–42, 49–50, 57–58, and 65–66).

In the first solo chorus, beginning at measure 73, Ray chooses a specific concept, utilizing more half notes on the downbeats, which establishes a particular rhythmic feeling (measures 73, 77, 81, 97, and 101). He begins to introduce triplets in the second solo chorus, adding them to the phrasing that he introduced during the head (measures 109, 117, 127–128, and 130).

As the piano solo reaches its zenith, at the beginning of the third solo chorus, the trio progresses to a walking feel that releases the tension built up over time. Listen to the way that Ray plays his quarter notes and continues to use rhythmic variations that maintain the new energy of the trio (measures 142, 144–145, 151–152, 155–156, and 161).

Ray's return to his initial rhythmic basis for the "head out" matches the band's diminuendo and the "calm at the end of the storm."

Have You Met Miss Jones?

The Oscar Peterson Trio's album *We Get Requests* is one of my absolute favorites for showcasing Ray Brown's bass sound. From the first time listening to him, I have felt that his tone is unparalleled in depth, color, thickness, warmth, and roundness.

On this track, despite the slow tempo of the song, Ray is able to maintain interest and intensity within a relaxed feeling. This performance demonstrates Ray's highly developed skill for balancing these equally important opposites.

Pay attention to the bass figure that occurs repeatedly during the "head" (measures 2, 10, 26, etc.). This figure, a real Ray Brown trademark, reappears again and again in Ray's playing, but in different variations and at different tempos.

Also notice the bass line at the end of the bridges (measures 23–24 and 71–72), where Ray creates melodic statements that both connect with the written melody and propel the tune forward. This concept—simultaneously leading and supporting—is crucial to understanding Ray Brown's playing.

How High the Moon

Here is one of my favorite performances by Ray with the original Oscar Peterson Trio (Herb Ellis, Oscar Peterson, and Ray Brown). This bass solo is considered by many to be one of the best, if not *the* best, bass solos ever recorded. It sure was difficult for me to learn, play, and notate—but well worth it!

Besides the obvious virtuosic technique that Ray displays, pay attention to his two-feel at the beginning (measures 25–27) and his progression into repeating the triplet figures hinted at right after (measures 29–30). This is another great example of how the bass can function as the foundation of the music, but can also urge it forward to maintain a sense of motion, movement, and dance.

After a relentlessly swinging accompaniment to Herb Ellis' guitar solo, Ray enters his solo by quoting the tune "They All Laughed" (measures 89–91). As if to remind us that his ability is no laughing matter, he then plays what is, to me, one of the most technically challenging and musically satisfying improvised bass solos on record.

Turn your attention to the lines found in measures 101–104 and 149–152 and notice how he maintains clear and complete musical statements, even at blistering velocity (measures 105–106, 143, and 146).

After this musical proclamation, rather than fading into the background, he jumps right back into his hard-driving, supportive role behind the piano solo and through to the end of the piece.

I'm an Old Cowhand (From the Rio Grande)

This is a compelling recording for several reasons. The first is that Ray is performing with saxophonist Sonny Rollins and drummer Shelly Manne—without a chordal instrument in the group. This arrangement of musicians provides both freedom and responsibility for all involved. Without a piano or guitar, there is generally more room for harmonic manipulation, but there is also the need to be very clear about one's intentions, as it may be more challenging to hear the intended harmony if the musicians do not execute their concepts clearly.

This is one area that Ray stood out above the crowd, especially during that period of bass playing. As Christian McBride, Wynton Marsalis, and many others have observed, Ray plays in a way that clearly defines the harmony and the listener therefore does not miss the chordal instrument. And more than that, he is able to seemingly anticipate where Sonny Rollins is going in his solo, as well as imply alternate harmonies (measures 80–81, 128, and 144–146). It should also be noted that the chords written in this transcription are based not only on the specific notes that Ray and Sonny play, but also the harmony that they allude to.

A second interesting factor is that much of the broad aspects of the performance and song are slightly off-balance, so to speak. The form of the song itself is unconventional: an eight-bar phrase followed by a 10-bar phrase, which equals one chorus. Shelly Manne's drum intro sets up a certain tongue-in-cheek feeling that can be heard throughout the song. Lastly, this composition is a bit askew from much of the standard repertoire of the time. All these factors, plus the format of the ensemble, add up to a recording that's slightly quirky, but also serious.

Of special note are Ray's musical conversation with Sonny in the first couple of choruses (measures 8–43) and his short but substantive solo (measures 116–152). He seems to capture this playfulness with a serious undertone that can be heard in the recording as a whole. See if you can hear the same.

I'm Glad There Is You (In This World of Ordinary People)

This ballad really allows us to relax into the typical command that Ray gives to the beat—the "stewardship of the quarter note," according to bassist Steve Kirby. At all times, even in a ballad with no drums, I have never found an instance where I could question the time or harmony in Ray's performances (measures 39–42).

While this bass line may not have a lot of notes, it can be an exciting challenge to play fewer notes well. One has to be unshakably confident in his or her ability; this conviction shines through when a great player has worked as hard as Ray did.

Another point of interest is the line at measure 62—not only for its unconventional fingering, but for how Herb Ellis and Stan Getz respond to this phrase that Ray starts. This is a small but very clear example of playing as a *unit*.

Killer Joe

This classic track from Quincy Jones' *Walking in Space* is a great example of Ray's inventiveness, freedom, and ability to play a wide variety of ideas over more static harmony.

With most of the song alternating between two chords, Ray demonstrates many options for creating bass lines in this scenario. Notice his many variations over these two chords in measures 5–8, 29–32, 61–62, 65–66, 69–72, and 129–130. The sheer number of different ways that he creates bass lines over these two repeating chords represents pure mastery and relentless creativity.

Note Ray's fluidity and control of the instrument through his use of triplets here; his movement up and down the instrument as he weaves these phrases is brilliant. Listen particularly to the velocity and precision of his triplet phrases in measures 79, 101–104, and 106 and try to emulate the command of the instrument that he displays.

Love Is Here to Stay

Here is an interesting example of Ray playing eighth notes in a way that represents how the somewhat elusive swing feel is notated. In other words, there is a consistent triplet-feel undercurrent in swung eighth notes. The second eighth (the "and" of a beat), is played in a way that is illustrated above, for the purposes of attempting to capture a feeling on paper. Ironically, a great many tempos and types of swing do not usually follow this ubiquitous notation.

In this recording, however, Ray plays his eighth notes in a way that best follows this conventional notation. His upbeats are really quite in sync with an undercurrent of triplets that are mostly felt, rather than played specifically (measures 3, 7, 9, 13, 15, 17, 19, 20, 30, 31, 35, 36, etc.). You can see that I have kept plain eighth notes in the transcription, rather than writing out every triplet.

And, once again, observe Ray's note choices. I just love the sound of the 3rd as a downbeat here (measures 37, 66, 68, and 82), especially when it is set up so well by previous notes in the bass line. We can learn so much from these subtle yet important choices that Ray made.

Mack the Knife

The genesis of this whole project was an experience with this exact recording. While at Berklee College of Music, my instructor, Whit Browne, played this cut for me in one of our private lessons. He pointed out the low F note on beat 3 of measure 9 and said, "That is the reason I started playing bass." Apparently, he was given this album as a gift as a young man. He had not yet started playing an instrument, but recognized the song title, so he chose to play that song first. As soon as he heard Ray declare that F, he immediately wanted to know what the instrument was, and then started his lifetime as a bassist. Whit's story inspired me, and what you see here is a direct result of his guidance and enthusiasm.

Check out the repeated notes at measure 41 and the subsequent ascending line (measures 41–46). This repetition of notes is a perfect example of what Ray himself called "spinning the wheels." This simple technique serves so many roles: providing harmonic and rhythmic tension; providing interest and variation at key points in the song structure; and grounding the ear to the key center, time, and group awareness. It is very much like a bow being pulled back to tension to release an arrow or, as Ray implies, gunning an engine before throwing a car into gear.

Study his relatively short but, to me, very hip solo. Notice that he chooses his notes based on the melodies that he is creating, not just the "correct" notes from corresponding chord scales (measures 117–118, 133–134).

Towards the end of the solo (measures 125–128), notice that his phrase goes down, then lower, goes back up, and, finally, higher again, generating a nice musical feeling of variety and question-and-answer. And ending with that blues feeling completes the solo perfectly (measures 135–136).

Moten Swing

If there is one clear example in these transcriptions that represents Ray's commanding sense of rhythmic time, this song is it. Measures 41–72 feature Ray in duet with saxophone master Sonny Stitt. Listening to this recording really helps us to understand the importance of dance in the feeling of swing.

Ray executes his bass line with deep swing, and also composes lines that add to the rhythmic intensity. Pay attention to the last two measures (71–72), where Ray plays notes that build the intensity for the entrance of Ed Thigpen's drums.

Look for examples in this piece of Ray's deviations from the chords (measures 78–79, 121–122, and 185–188), his maneuvering through common chord progressions, and his rhythmic accents that flesh out the music (measures 96, 133–134, and 223–224).

Night Train

In 2013, as this book was being written, we lost the great American author Albert Murray. His thoughts and analysis on jazz, the blues, and the human condition as an African-American will continue to resonate for years to come with books such as *Stomping the Blues* and *The Omni-Americans*. In an interview about his work *The Blue Devils of Nada*, he said: "What we do when we play the blues is precisely that: we play with the blues, we stomp the blues. We get rid of the blues. So that blues music is goodtime music because it dispels the menacing elements in the environment or at least it holds them at bay so we can get on with the human proposition. How do you beat the blues? By elegance. You don't beat the blues—it's that insouciance, it's that 'don't care if I' elegance that defeats the blues."

This recording of "Night Train" summarizes all of these elements: elegance, the blues as sadness, and a "goodtime" response to that sadness. And, for me, a definitive way to express these elements is through the type of articulations and note choices that Ray makes, especially in his solo (measures 59–84).

With "blue notes"—the ♭3rd, ♭5th, or ♭7th—played against a major tonality (measures 59–61, 64, 73, 75, 79, and 81–84); sliding into and out of notes during the melody (measures 4, 8, and 12) and throughout the solo; call and response (measures 73–80); and rhythmic manipulation (measures 80–81); Ray condenses many of the vocal-like devices that bring the blues to life in just two short choruses.

When you listen to his walking lines, see if you also hear the "don't care if I" attitude that Mr. Murray speaks of. What I notice is a combination of confidence, flexibility, fluidity, and clarity of purpose that encapsulates all that the blues signifies.

Sometimes I'm Happy

Besides "swinging to the hardest degree," another phrase that comes to mind when I listen to this performance is "full of life." It is as if Ray's instrument is glowing, burning, about to take off in flight. The conviction and relentless energy that he uses to address this song typifies the feeling that we, as musicians, should aspire to bring into our own playing.

Listen to Ray's two-feel in measures 9–11, 17–18, 29–30, 45–48, and 53–56. This feeling that he evokes provides buoyancy and forward movement without adding clutter.

There is a nice example of Ray's facility in thumb position later in the piece (measures 382–384) and it's a pleasure to hear the trio play hits in the last chorus (measures 393–396) in lieu of playing the theme out, which is a simple and elegant arranging choice. The listener may perceive a sense of arrival and a setup to the completion of the song without the convention of the "head out."

Ray's solo here can either be the icing or the cake itself, depending on your perspective. From the opening salvo, you can sample a Ray blues cliché (measures 235–236). Do your best to imitate Ray's feeling, as well as the notes and his sound. It is these subtle articulations that not only define Ray, but are the essence of authentic musical expression.

Examples of the kind of articulation I am speaking of occur in many places in the solo: note the upward scoops (measures 243 and 262), the hammered-on slurs (measures 247–248, 293, and 305), and the fall-offs (measures 254, 259, and 314). These are just a very few places where small devices make all the difference in a quality performance.

The Surrey with the Fringe on Top

I enjoy these *Poll Winners* recordings that Ray did because his big sound is usually easy to hear clearly and the arrangements that the musicians wrote tend to sound more playful and free when compared to conventional record dates. Ray is allowed many instances to shine, and this song is a great example of that.

The lines he creates in the intro (measures 9–16) are both enjoyable to play and to listen to and have a depth of content that retains their musical integrity. Ray gets to play the main part of the melody (measures 29–44, 53–63, and 233–240) and improvises an absorbing counterpoint to the melody at the bridge (measures 45–52).

This song also features several Ray specialties: using 10ths for color (measure 70), triplet drops while "raking" the strings (measure 71), and "clef diving" (measures 105–108), where Ray will slowly build his line higher and higher and then suddenly dive down several octaves for a very satisfying tension-and-release moment.

His phrases between the ensemble hits (measures 141–144, 149–160, and 165–172) are my favorite kind of combination of bebop lines and a blues sound or feeling. Notice how he maintains interest in the song by providing some musical moments for the whole trio in what would normally be just a solo section.

Tune Up

In this trio setting, led by pianist Monty Alexander, Ray teaches us about playing up-tempo tunes, or "upstairs." This is also a lesson on forethought in creating improvised bass lines. At such a quick pace, we should strive to think and adjust rapidly and prepare our next move ahead of time.

Ray demonstrates this in every performance, but particularly here. Look at and listen to the end of measures, specifically when a chord change is about to happen. You will notice that Ray chooses very strong and logical approach notes that keep the song cohesive, even at this tempo (measures 98, 130, 167, and 181).

Also, note his two-feel when the song changes meter (measures 65–68 and 81–84). Ray's simple, grounded notes clearly define the harmony and propel the rhythm. Rather than adding perhaps unnecessary rhythmic figures, he maintains consistently strong half notes, which serve this particular recording in the best way possible.

Up There

When I listen to this piece written by Ray, I hear an energy and a sense of excitement that is infectious. Phineas Newborn's piano introduction alone is considered by great pianists to be very valuable, and the entire ensemble plays with confidence and conviction. As I mentioned in "Tune Up," jazz musicians often refer to fast tunes as being "up" or "upstairs" and I imagine that the title of this song must be referring to its very fast tempo.

There is a certain perspective that believes that one criterion for creating good bass lines is that each beat should contain a different note. In this way of thinking, repeated notes are to be avoided. To me, though, there are circumstances and scenarios when repeated notes sound great and serve the music very well. This bass line of Ray's is a great example of using repeated notes intelligently.

Consider the fast tempo, the velocity of the rhythms, and the high energy of this recording. I think that it's very logical to play repetitive bass notes or phrases that ground the song, reinforce the harmony, and allow for smooth execution on Ray's part.

Speaking from personal experience, playing fast tunes requires one to develop new strengths by combining core skills at these elevated tempos. The principles are all the same: play in tune, have a good sound and a good feel, play good notes, play well with the other musicians. But now we're sometimes doing so at breakneck speeds, which is often not something we're familiar with. Note how successfully Ray applies these principles here, in spite of the tempo.

Also note the different harmony that Ray implies, substituting a dominant sound over a previously established major chord (measures 89, 125, and 153) and several times hinting at an F minor chord instead of the tonic A♭ (measures 73, 97, and 225).

This performance of Ray's can serve as one strong example of how to play bass lines at fast tempos, as well as an example of how repeated notes and repeated patterns can suit a given musical situation very well.

Autumn in New York

Words and Music by Vernon Duke

Ella and Louis Again
Verve 825 374-2

Custard Puff

By Ray Brown

*Played behind the beat.

26

Days of Wine and Roses

Lyrics by Johnny Mercer
Music by Henry Mancini

Ray Brown Trio - *Black Orpheus*
Evidence ECD 22076-2

*Played behind the beat.

*Slap strings against fingerboard.

*Played behind the beat.

Easy Does It

Words and Music by Sy Oliver and Jimmy Young

The Oscar Peterson Trio - *Night Train*
Verve 821 724-2

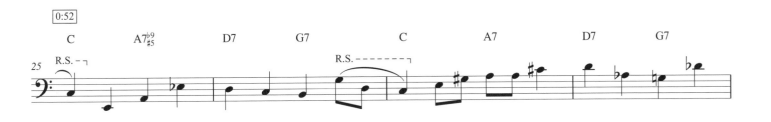

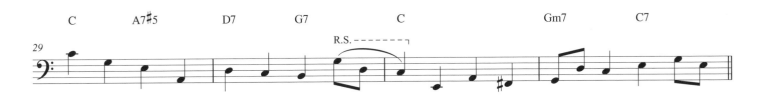

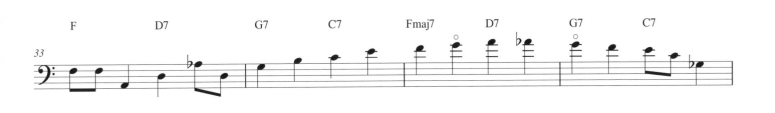

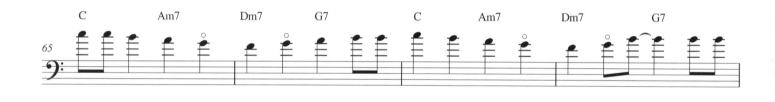

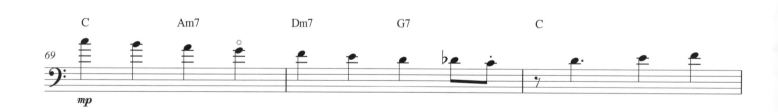

Gravy Waltz

Lyrics by Steve Allen
Music by Ray Brown

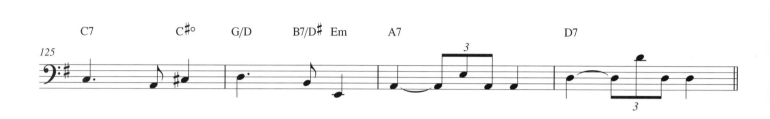

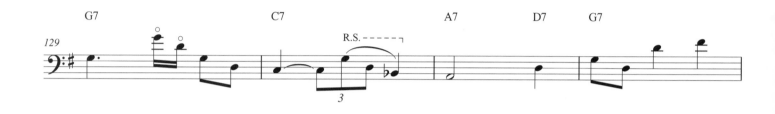

2:45

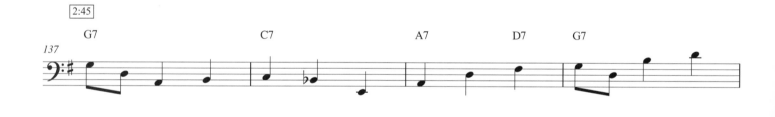

Have You Met Miss Jones?

Words by Lorenz Hart
Music by Richard Rodgers

The Oscar Peterson Trio - *We Get Requests*
Verve 810 047-2

How High the Moon

Lyrics by Nancy Hamilton
Music by Morgan Lewis

The Oscar Peterson Trio at the Stratford Shakespearean Festival
Verve 314 513 752-2

*Played behind the beat.

*Played behind the beat.

I'm an Old Cowhand
(From the Rio Grande)

Words and Music by Johnny Mercer

Sonny Rollins - *Way Out West*
OJCCD-337-2

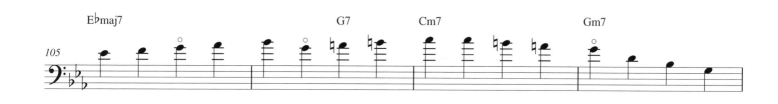

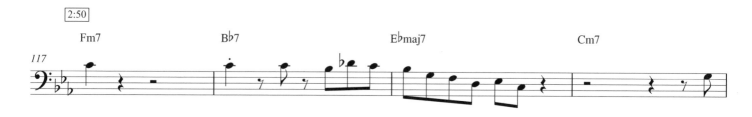

59

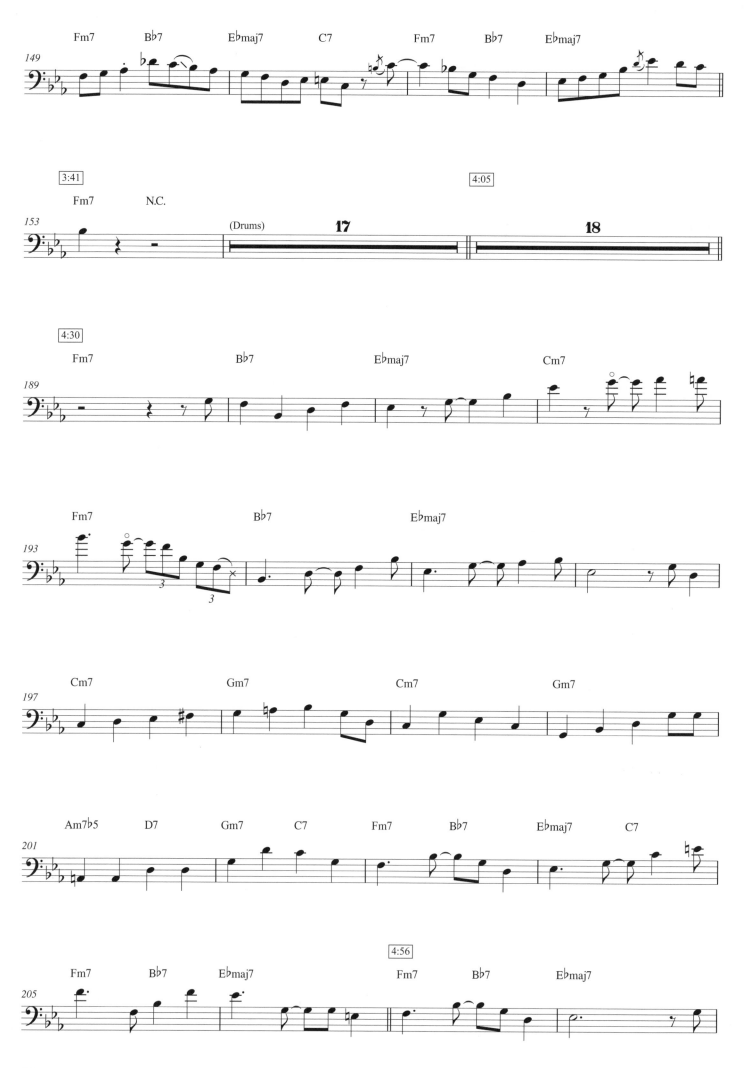

I'm Glad There Is You
(In This World of Ordinary People)

Words and Music by Paul Madeira and Jimmy Dorsey

Stan Getz and The Oscar Peterson Trio
Verve 827 826-2

Moderately slow Ballad ♩ = 70

Killer Joe

By Benny Golson

Love Is Here to Stay

Music and Lyrics by George Gershwin and Ira Gershwin

Ella and Louis Again
Verve 825 374-2

Mack the Knife

English Words by Marc Blitzstein
Original German Words by Bert Brecht
Music by Kurt Weill

Moten Swing

By Buster Moten and Bennie Moten

Sonny Stitt Sits in with the Oscar Peterson Trio
Verve 849 396-2

Night Train

Words by Oscar Washington and Lewis C. Simpkins
Music by Jimmy Forrest

Oscar Peterson Trio - *Night Train*
Verve 821 724-2

Sometimes I'm Happy

Words by Clifford Grey and Irving Caesar
Music by Vincent Youmans

Oscar Peterson Trio - *The Trio: Live from Chicago*
Verve 314 539 063-2

The Surrey with the Fringe on Top

Lyrics by Oscar Hammerstein II
Music by Richard Rodgers

The Poll Winners Ride Again!
OJCCD 607-25

*Chord symbols reflect implied harmony, next 20 meas.

*Played straight.

*Played behind the beat.

Tune Up

By Miles Davis

Monty Alexander - *Facets*
Concord CCD-4108

Up There

By Ray Brown

Teddy Edwards/Howard McGhee - *Together Again!!!!*
OJCCD 424-25

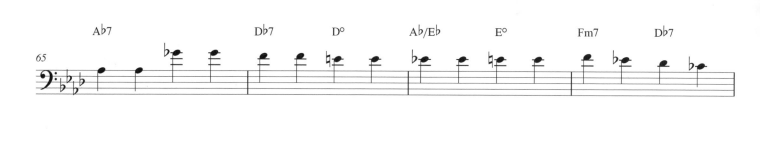

BASS NOTATION LEGEND

THE MUSICAL STAFF shows pitches and rhythms and is divided by bar lines into measures. Pitches are named after the first seven letters of the alphabet.

Notes:

HAMMER-ON: Strike the first (lower) note with one finger, then sound the higher note (on the same string) without picking by pressing it down firmly with another finger.

PULL-OFF: Place both fingers on the notes to be sounded. Strike the first note and without picking, pull the finger off to sound the second (lower) note.

LEGATO SLIDE: Strike the first note and then slide the same fret-hand finger up or down to the second note. The second note is not struck.

SHIFT SLIDE: Same as legato slide, except the second note is struck.

SCOOP: A short, quick slide up to a note, approaching from below.

FALL-OFF: A short, quick slide down from a note after striking.

MUTED STRINGS: A percussive sound is produced by laying the left hand across the string(s) and striking them as normal with the right hand.

HARMONIC: Strike the note while the left hand lightly touches the string directly over the note location indicated.

RAKE: Drag the right hand picking finger across the strings indicated with a single motion.

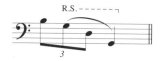

Additional Musical Definitions

(accent) • Accentuate note (play it louder).

(staccato) • Play the note shorter.

(accent) • Accentuate note with great intensity.

(tenuto) • Hold the note for its full value.

ACKNOWLEDGMENTS

Many thanks to John Clayton, Christian McBride, Wynton Marsalis, Loren Schoenberg, Justin Varnes, Paul Sikivie, Michael Blanco, Chris Biesterfeldt, Tom McEvoy, Ethan Mann, Marco Panascia, Yasushi Nakamura, Ulysses Owens, Jr., and Oscar Perez for their incredibly invaluable assistance with this book.

Musical thanks to Ray Brown, Reginald Veal, Rodney Whitaker, Ben Wolfe, Whit Browne, John Repucci, Wycliffe Gordon, Victor Goines, Marc Cary, Terell Stafford, Eric Reed, and Benny Green for their inspiration and instruction.

Additional thanks to Upton Bass and Pirastro Strings for their endorsements.

Thank you to my family and friends, who have been an unending source of joy: Jim and Jen Rybicki; Caroline, Bean, Shel, Jeff, Becky, Asher, Isla, Steve, Brooke, and Ted Smith; Tom, Denise, Celeste, and Jon Rybicki; P.J. Santoro; Greg, Jessica, Aidan, and Abigail McMillan; Joe McGlone and Stephanie Rybicki; Dave, Peg, D.J., Adrienne, Dan, Andrea, Aaron, Tiffany, Caleb Kruzer and Liana Nikkel; Mike, Amy, and Elsa Richmond; Mike, Tara, Jason, Amanda, Kevin, and Brandi Rybicki; Ray, Monica, Harrison, and Helena Stadnik; Ani Ngawang Palmo Rybicki; Matt, Jane, Julianna, and Elizabeth Coleman; Joe, Kim, and Eleanor Rybicki; Jason, Tina, and Josh Luboski; Brian Hegedus; and Mike, Kim, and Ethan Ventresca.

And very special thanks to my wife, Megan Buzzard Rybicki, who is patient, kind, and is a blessing in my life.

ABOUT THE AUTHOR

Raised in Cleveland, Ohio, Matthew Rybicki has performed with Wynton Marsalis and the Lincoln Center Jazz Orchestra, Wycliffe Gordon, Nnenna Freelon, Marcus Printup, Renee Fleming, Terell Stafford, Walter Blanding, Jr., Winard Harper, Mark Whitfield, and Victor Goines. He has also had the great fortune of performing at many well-respected venues in New York such as the Village Vanguard and the Blue Note, as well as concert halls and festivals in locations ranging from Africa to the Middle East and Italy to Taiwan. Rybicki maintains an active performing schedule, working with his own ensembles and with many accomplished colleagues and mentors such as Lew Tabackin, Ulysses Owens, Jr., Christian Sands, Lewis Nash, Dan Nimmer, Oscar Perez, David Berger, Charenee Wade, and Loren Schoenberg.

An adept educator, Matthew is an artist/instructor for Jazz at Lincoln Center, where he developed and taught the inaugural bass course in their Essentially Ellington Band Director Academy. He has also been the music director for several educational performance initiatives, including Jazz in the Schools and hospital tours in conjunction with Lincoln Center's Department of Programs for People with Disabilities. In addition, Rybicki was a coordinator for school programs by Midori and Friends and has led musical workshops at The Whitney Museum of American Art and the Guggenheim that connect jazz with visual art. He has also led clinics at the 2013 International Society of Bassists Convention, Georgia State University, as well as schools in New York City; Aspen, Colorado; St. Louis, Missouri; Cleveland, Ohio; and throughout the northeast.

With his debut CD, Driven, Matthew has formally entered the jazz scene as a performer and composer of note. Recording with jazz greats Ron Blake, Freddie Hendrix, Gerald Clayton, and Ulysses Owens, he was able to capture innovative and sophisticated performances with newly created original works that maintain ties to the history of jazz.

Matthew received his Bachelor of Music Degree from Berklee College of Music in 1995 and his Artist Diploma from the Juilliard School in 2004.

www.matthewrybicki.com

Photo by Sequoyah Daniel

Jazz Instruction & Improvisation

BOOKS FOR ALL INSTRUMENTS FROM HAL LEONARD

AN APPROACH TO JAZZ IMPROVISATION
by Dave Pozzi
Musicians Institute Press
Explore the styles of Charlie Parker, Sonny Rollins, Bud Powell and others with this comprehensive guide to jazz improvisation. Covers: scale choices • chord analysis • phrasing • melodies • harmonic progressions • more.
00695135 Book/CD Pack.......................$17.95

THE ART OF MODULATING
FOR PIANISTS AND JAZZ MUSICIANS
by Carlos Salzedo &
Lucile Lawrence
Schirmer
The Art of Modulating is a treatise originally intended for the harp, but this edition has been edited for use by intermediate keyboardists and other musicians who have an understanding of basic music theory. In its pages you will find: table of intervals; modulation rules; modulation formulas; examples of modulation; extensions and cadences; ten fragments of dances; five characteristic pieces; and more.
50490581 ....$19.99

BUILDING A JAZZ VOCABULARY
By Mike Steinel
A valuable resource for learning the basics of jazz from Mike Steinel of the University of North Texas. It covers: the basics of jazz • how to build effective solos • a comprehensive practice routine • and a jazz vocabulary of the masters.
00849911 ....$19.95

THE CYCLE OF FIFTHS
by Emile and Laura De Cosmo
This essential instruction book provides more than 450 exercises, including hundreds of melodic and rhythmic ideas. The book is designed to help improvisors master the cycle of fifths, one of the primary progressions in music. Guaranteed to refine technique, enhance improvisational fluency, and improve sight-reading!
00311114 ....$16.99

THE DIATONIC CYCLE
by Emile and Laura De Cosmo
Renowned jazz educators Emile and Laura De Cosmo provide more than 300 exercises to help improvisors tackle one of music's most common progressions: the diatonic cycle. This book is guaranteed to refine technique, enhance improvisational fluency, and improve sight-reading!
00311115 ....$16.95

EAR TRAINING
by Keith Wyatt,
Carl Schroeder and Joe Elliott
Musicians Institute Press
Covers: basic pitch matching • singing major and minor scales • identifying intervals • transcribing melodies and rhythm • identifying chords and progressions • seventh chords and the blues • modal interchange, chromaticism, modulation • and more.
00695198 Book/2-CD Pack $24.95

EXERCISES AND ETUDES FOR THE JAZZ INSTRUMENTALIST
by J.J. Johnson
Designed as study material and playable by any instrument, these pieces run the gamut of the jazz experience, featuring common and uncommon time signatures and keys, and styles from ballads to funk. They are progressively graded so that both beginners and professionals will be challenged by the demands of this wonderful music.
00842018 Bass Clef Edition $16.95
00842042 Treble Clef Edition $16.95

JAZZOLOGY
THE ENCYCLOPEDIA OF JAZZ THEORY FOR ALL MUSICIANS
by Robert Rawlins and
Nor Eddine Bahha
This comprehensive resource covers a variety of jazz topics, for beginners and pros of any instrument. The book serves as an encyclopedia for reference, a thorough methodology for the student, and a workbook for the classroom.
00311167 ....$19.99

JAZZ THEORY RESOURCES
by Bert Ligon
Houston Publishing, Inc.
This is a jazz theory text in two volumes. **Volume 1 includes**: review of basic theory • rhythm in jazz performance • triadic generalization • diatonic harmonic progressions and analysis • substitutions and turnarounds • and more. **Volume 2 includes**: modes and modal frameworks • quartal harmony • extended tertian structures and triadic superimposition • pentatonic applications • coloring "outside" the lines and beyond • and more.
00030458 Volume 1 ....$39.95
00030459 Volume 2 ....$29.95

JOY OF IMPROV
by Dave Frank
and John Amaral
This book/CD course on improvisation for all instruments and all styles will help players develop monster musical skills! Book One imparts a solid basis in technique, rhythm, chord theory, ear training and improv concepts. **Book Two** explores more advanced chord voicings, chord arranging techniques and more challenging blues and melodic lines. The CD can be used as a listening and play-along tool.
00220005 Book 1 – Book/CD Pack.......................$27.99
00220006 Book 2 – Book/CD Pack.......................$26.99

THE PATH TO JAZZ IMPROVISATION
by Emile and Laura De Cosmo
This fascinating jazz instruction book offers an innovative, scholarly approach to the art of improvisation. It includes in-depth analysis and lessons about: cycle of fifths • diatonic cycle • overtone series • pentatonic scale • harmonic and melodic minor scale • polytonal order of keys • blues and bebop scales • modes • and more.
00310904 ....$14.99

THE SOURCE
THE DICTIONARY OF CONTEMPORARY AND TRADITIONAL SCALES
by Steve Barta
This book serves as an informative guide for people who are looking for good, solid information regarding scales, chords, and how they work together. It provides right and left hand fingerings for scales, chords, and complete inversions. Includes over 20 different scales, each written in all 12 keys.
00240885 ....$18.99

21 BEBOP EXERCISES
by Steve Rawlins
This book/CD pack is both a warm-up collection and a manual for bebop phrasing. Its tasty and sophisticated exercises will help you develop your proficiency with jazz interpretation. It concentrates on practice in all twelve keys – moving higher by half-step – to help develop dexterity and range. The companion CD includes all of the exercises in 12 keys.
00315341 Book/CD Pack....................................$17.95

HAL•LEONARD®
CORPORATION
7777 W. BLUEMOUND RD. P.O. BOX 13819 MILWAUKEE, WI 53213

Visit Hal Leonard online at
www.halleonard.com

Prices, contents & availability subject to change without notice.

0113

The Best-Selling Jazz Book of All Time Is Now Legal!

The Real Books are the most popular jazz books of all time. Since the 1970s, musicians have trusted these volumes to get them through every gig, night after night. The problem is that the books were illegally produced and distributed, without any regard to copyright law, or royalties paid to the composers who created these musical masterpieces.

Hal Leonard is very proud to present the first legitimate and legal editions of these books ever produced. You won't even notice the difference, other than all the notorious errors being fixed: the covers and typeface look the same, the song lists are nearly identical, and the price for our edition is even cheaper than the originals!

Every conscientious musician will appreciate that these books are now produced accurately and ethically, benefitting the songwriters that we owe for some of the greatest tunes of all time!

Also available:

00240264	The Real Blues Book	$34.99
00310910	The Real Bluegrass Book	$29.99
00240440	The Trane Book	$22.99
00240137	Miles Davis Real Book	$19.95
00240355	The Real Dixieland Book	$29.99
00122335	The Real Dixieland Book B♭ Edition	$29.99
00240235	The Duke Ellington Real Book	$19.99
00240268	The Real Jazz Solos Book	$30.00
00240348	The Real Latin Book	$35.00
00127107	The Real Latin Book B♭ Edition	$35.00
00240358	The Charlie Parker Real Book	$19.99
00240331	The Bud Powell Real Book	$19.99
00240437	The Real R&B Book	$39.99
00240313	The Real Rock Book	$35.00
00240323	The Real Rock Book – Vol. 2	$35.00
00240359	The Real Tab Book	$32.50
00240317	The Real Worship Book	$29.99

THE REAL CHRISTMAS BOOK

00240306	C Edition	$29.99
00240345	B♭ Edition	$29.99
00240346	E♭ Edition	$29.99
00240347	Bass Clef Edition	$29.99
00240431	A-G CD Backing Tracks	$24.99
00240432	H-M CD Backing Tracks	$24.99
00240433	N-Y CD Backing Tracks	$24.99

THE REAL VOCAL BOOK

00240230	Volume 1 High Voice	$35.00
00240307	Volume 1 Low Voice	$35.00
00240231	Volume 2 High Voice	$35.00
00240308	Volume 2 Low Voice	$35.00
00240391	Volume 3 High Voice	$35.00
00240392	Volume 3 Low Voice	$35.00
00118318	Volume 4 High Voice	$35.00
00118319	Volume 4 Low Voice	$35.00

THE REAL BOOK – STAFF PAPER

00240327		$10.99

HOW TO PLAY FROM A REAL BOOK

FOR ALL MUSICIANS
by Robert Rawlins

00312097		$17.50

VOLUME 1

00240221	C Edition	$35.00
00240224	B♭ Edition	$35.00
00240225	E♭ Edition	$35.00
00240226	Bass Clef Edition	$35.00
00240292	C Edition 6 x 9	$30.00
00240339	B♭ Edition 6 x 9	$30.00
00451087	C Edition on CD-ROM	$25.00
00240302	A-D CD Backing Tracks	$24.99
00240303	E-J CD Backing Tracks	$24.95
00240304	L-R CD Backing Tracks	$24.95
00240305	S-Z CD Backing Tracks	$24.99
00110604	Book/USB Flash Drive Backing Tracks Pack	$79.99
00110599	USB Flash Drive Only	$50.00

VOLUME 2

00240222	C Edition	$35.50
00240227	B♭ Edition	$35.00
00240228	E♭ Edition	$35.00
00240229	Bass Clef Edition	$35.00
00240293	C Edition 6 x 9	$30.00
00125900	B♭ Edition 6 x 9	$30.00
00451088	C Edition on CD-ROM	$27.99
00240351	A-D CD Backing Tracks	$24.99
00240352	E-I CD Backing Tracks	$24.99
00240353	J-R CD Backing Tracks	$24.99
00240354	S-Z CD Backing Tracks	$24.99

VOLUME 3

00240233	C Edition	$35.00
00240284	B♭ Edition	$35.00
00240285	E♭ Edition	$35.00
00240286	Bass Clef Edition	$35.00
00240338	C Edition 6 x 9	$30.00
00451089	C Edition on CD-ROM	$29.99

VOLUME 4

00240296	C Edition	$35.00
00103348	B♭ Edition	$35.00
00103349	E♭ Edition	$35.00
00103350	Bass Clef Edition	$35.00

VOLUME 5

00240349	C Edition	$35.00

Complete song lists online at www.halleonard.com
Prices, content, and availability subject to change without notice.

HAL•LEONARD®
CORPORATION
7777 W. BLUEMOUND RD. P.O. BOX 13819 MILWAUKEE, WI 53213

1214